Jimmy's Frog

A Picture Story of Prepositions

By Mary Meyers, Illustrated by Stephen Garry

Copyright, Revised Edition, 2013,   ISBN 978-0-9687377-9-8

This resource is reproducible for the purchaser's class only.

It is not to be loaned out or shared with teachers.

Jimmy's Frog
A Book of Prepositions

Synopsis

This is the story of a little boy who catches a frog as he plays down at the creek. He then decides to go back home and show it off to his friends. To get back home, the little boy goes up the hill, and down the hill, across a log, through a tunnel, under a fence and over the fence, behind the bushes and beside the train tracks. Finally, as the little guy crosses between the white lines to join his buddies, his wee frog makes a getaway by jumping out of his pocket. Of course to get back to his home at the creek, our wee froggie has to return by the same route, but in reverse.

At the end of the story, the little boy's friends think that he is telling a fib, and the frog sits on a lily pad, thrilled to be safe at home.

* Your story can be as easy or as detailed as your class can comprehend. Rereadings will extend students' comprehension of the concepts and descriptions.

* Prepositions of place are provided to post on the board. Word cards for verbs and outdoor vocabulary are included.

* Students are immersed in active, joyful listening tasks, as well as reading and writing activities.

How To Use
Jimmy's Frog
A Book of Prepositions

- Copy the picture story and staple it into a book.
- As you show the pictures, tell the story in your own words.
- Use the names of students in your class to personalize it.
- Embellish the story however you wish.

  i.e., One hot, Saturday morning Jimmy was bored . . .
      . . . but then froggie bumped his head on the fence;
      Mother frog started calling her baby, . . .
      "Help!" he called," I'm stuck. Help me, please."
- Introduce the prepositions of place as you attach the
  pictures and word cards to the board.
- Say and have students repeat, and/or read out the list.
- Have students complete the worksheets.
- Another day, reread the story adding new detail and/or
  asking students to tell what's happening in the picture.
- Review the preposition list & add verbs & outdoor words.
- Each student gets a copy of the story and is asked to
  sequence the pictures and write the page numbers.
- Teach cohesive devices; next, then, after that, finally
- During retellings add descriptive words and feelings
  to enrich the characters and storyline.
- Students write the story in their own words.

Writing Sequence – Words to Discourse

1. Write the proposition under each picture.

2. Write words for nouns in the picture.

   i.e., water, boy, frog, tree, flower, etc.

3. Add adjectives for the noun words.

   i.e., little, green frog, yellow flower, etc.

4. Write your story under the pictures.

Teaching Prepositions

Prepositions tell space and time; they also include idiomatic and special uses. Teach older students temporal prepositions and idiomatic uses at another time.

Spacial Examples

in, on, above, under, underneath, beneath, below, over, here, there, near, far, beside, next to, between, behind, around, off, through, across, the edge of, the middle of, in front of, center, to, from, along, toward

Temporal Examples

after, before, until, about, at, during, ago, for (6 hours), since, by (midnight), etc.

Examples of Idiomatic and Special Uses

for (name), instead of, because of, in spite of, in charge of, with, in control of, with regards to, besides that, etc.

up	down
over	under
beside	out of
across	in

in between

behind

into

through

water creek

hill	bushes
log	fence
train tracks	
tunnel	tree

pocket

horse

frog

friends

rocks

flowers

1. Write where.

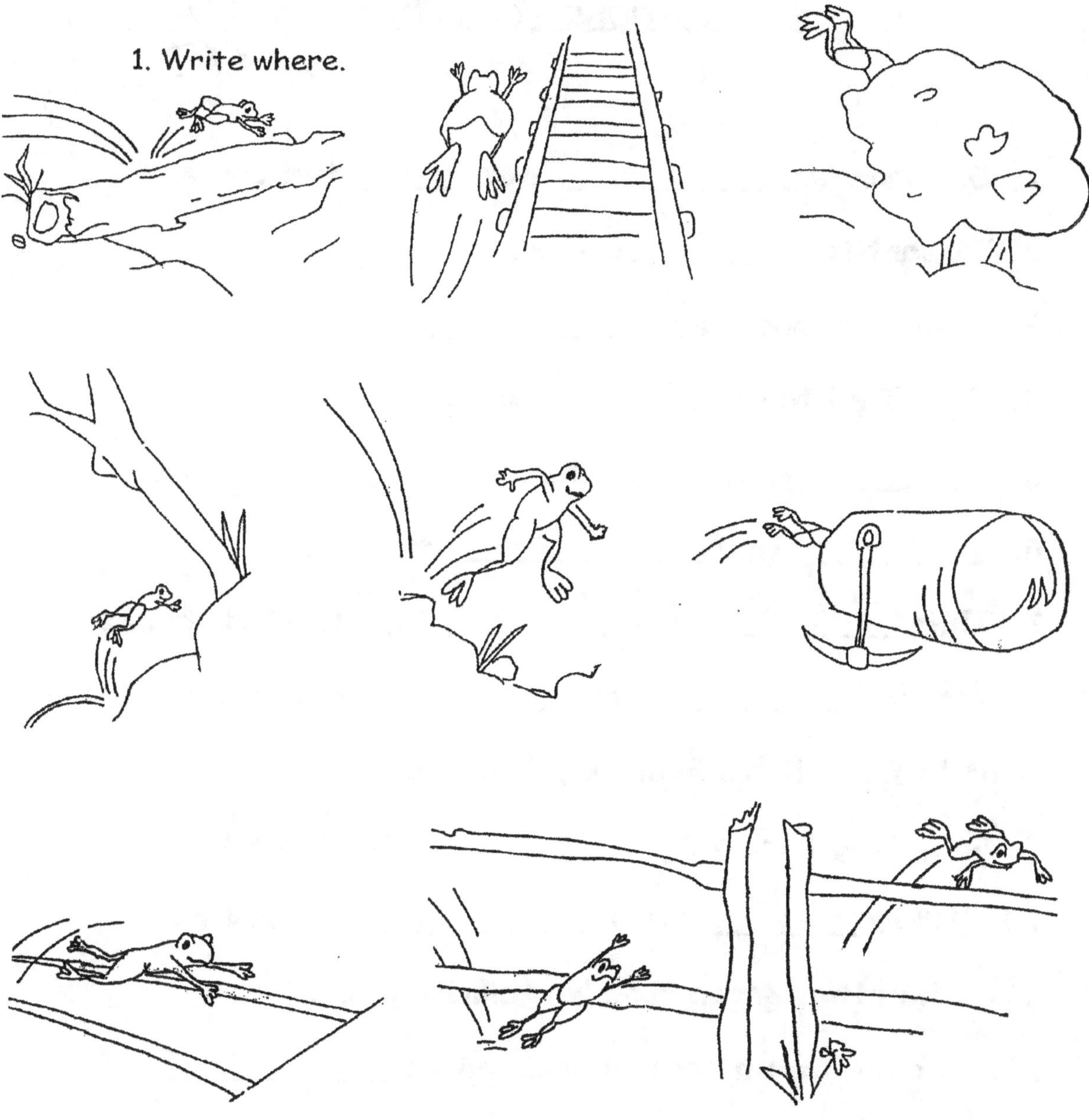

up the hill   down the hill   across the log

through the tunnel   behind the bushes

over the fence   under the fence

beside the train tracks   between the white lines

<u>Prepositions Tell Where</u>

1. One morning, ______________ was ______ the creek.

2. "I want to __________ a frog."

3. "I want to show my ______________."

4. Frog liked to swim ________ the water.

5. ____________ went ______ the hill and __________ the hill.

6. ____________ went ______________ the log.

7. Then ____________ went ______________ the dark tunnel.

8. When ____________ went ____________ the fence,

   little frog hit his head. Ouch! Watch out!

9. Baby frog tried to get __________ of the pocket.

10. When __________ went ____________ the bushes,

    the little, green frog was climbing out.

11. I didn't see a train, but I walked ______________

    the tracks just to be safe.

12. When __________ walked ____________ the two,

    white lines, the little frog jumped ________ and

    ran all the way home.

Draw a box beside each word. Add a happy face/arrow for each preposition.

up

down

in

outside

on

under

below

through

across

behind

beside

between

in front of

middle of

center of

top

bottom

right

left

off

here

there

around

upside down

The Frog Story

Cut out the sentences and sequence them.

Jimmy turned around to go back home.

He jumped into the water with a splash.

He caught the frog and put him in his pocket.

Frog hit his head on the fence. Ouch! That hurt.

One day, Jimmy was playing down at the creek.

Jimmy had to go up the big hill.

Then he went behind the bushes.

Frog jumped out of Jimmy's pocket.

Jimmy went through a dark tunnel.

"Where's the frog Jimmy?" said his friends.

Jimmy crossed the street to see his friends.

Frog ran so fast - all the way back home.

Frog is happy and Jimmy is sad.

Prepositions Tell Where

Draw a picture and write an idea.

across the _________   across the _________

beside the _______   beside the _______   beside the _______

through the _________   through the _________

behind the _______   behind the _______   behind the _______

Questions

1. What color is a frog? _______________________________

2. What colors can water be? _______________________

3. What color is a bulrush? _______________________

4. What color can the sky be?_______________________

5. What is a creek?_______________________________

6. What is a stream?_______________________________

7. What is a river? _______________________________

8. What is a lake? _______________________________

9. What is a Life Cycle? _______________________

10. What is a reptile? _______________________

11. Draw pictures of the frog's Life Cycle.

12. What is an insect? _______________________

13. Draw pictures of a butterfly's Life Cycle?

14. What is a mammal? _______________________

Internet Search

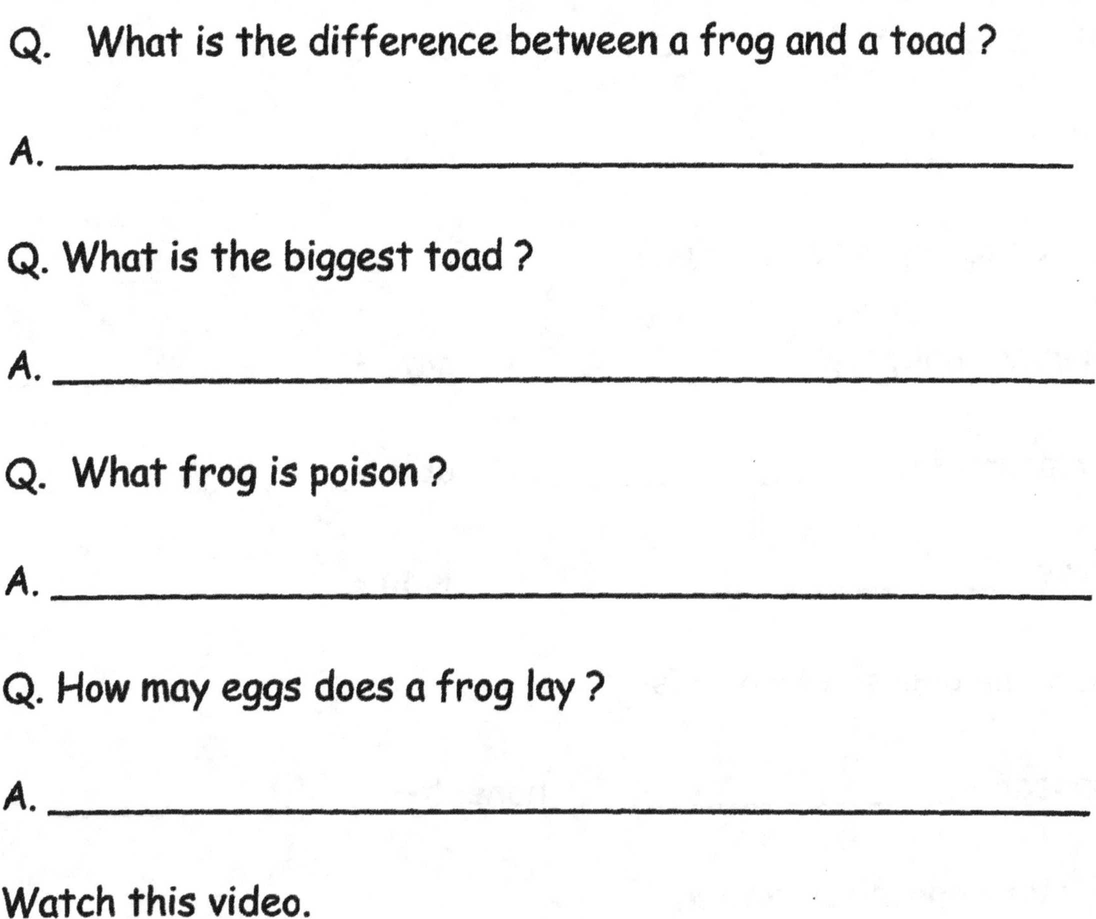

Ask and answer these questions. Q and A

Q. What is the difference between a frog and a toad ?

A. ____

Q. What is the biggest toad ?

A. ____

Q. What frog is poison ?

A. ____

Q. How may eggs does a frog lay ?

A. ____

Watch this video.

http://www.youtube.com/watch?v=oUBwBWC2oWQ

Opposites

1. Translate the word 'opposite'.
2. Now write the opposite of these words.

up __________   in __________   push __________   big __________

play __________   boy __________   win __________

3. Make opposites with **un-**

happy - unhappy   safe - __________

comfortable - __________   able - __________

true - __________   kind - __________

4. Make opposites with **dis-**

appear – __________   honest – __________

5. Make opposites with **in-**

complete - __________   visible - __________

Jimmy's
Frog

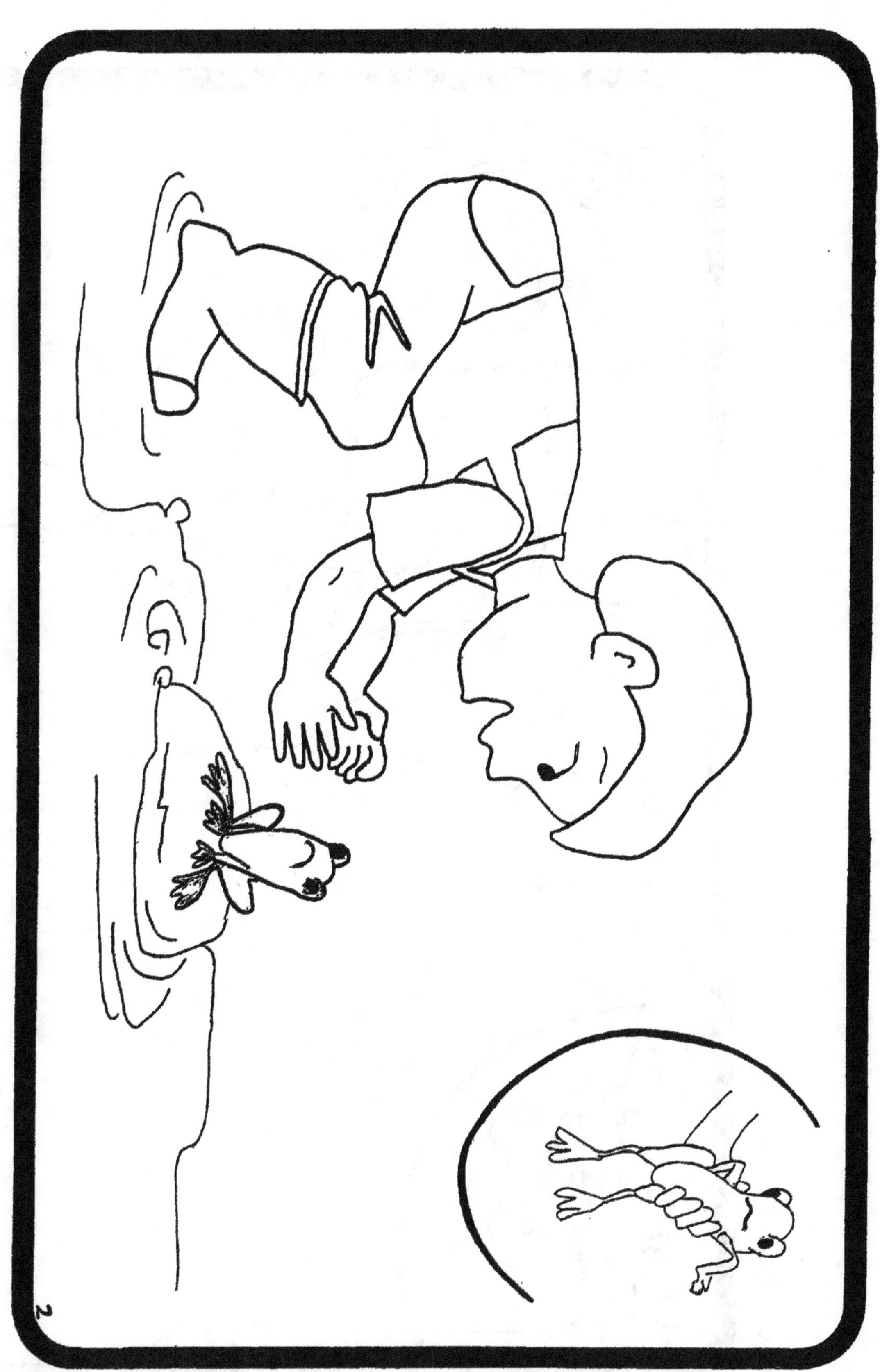

6

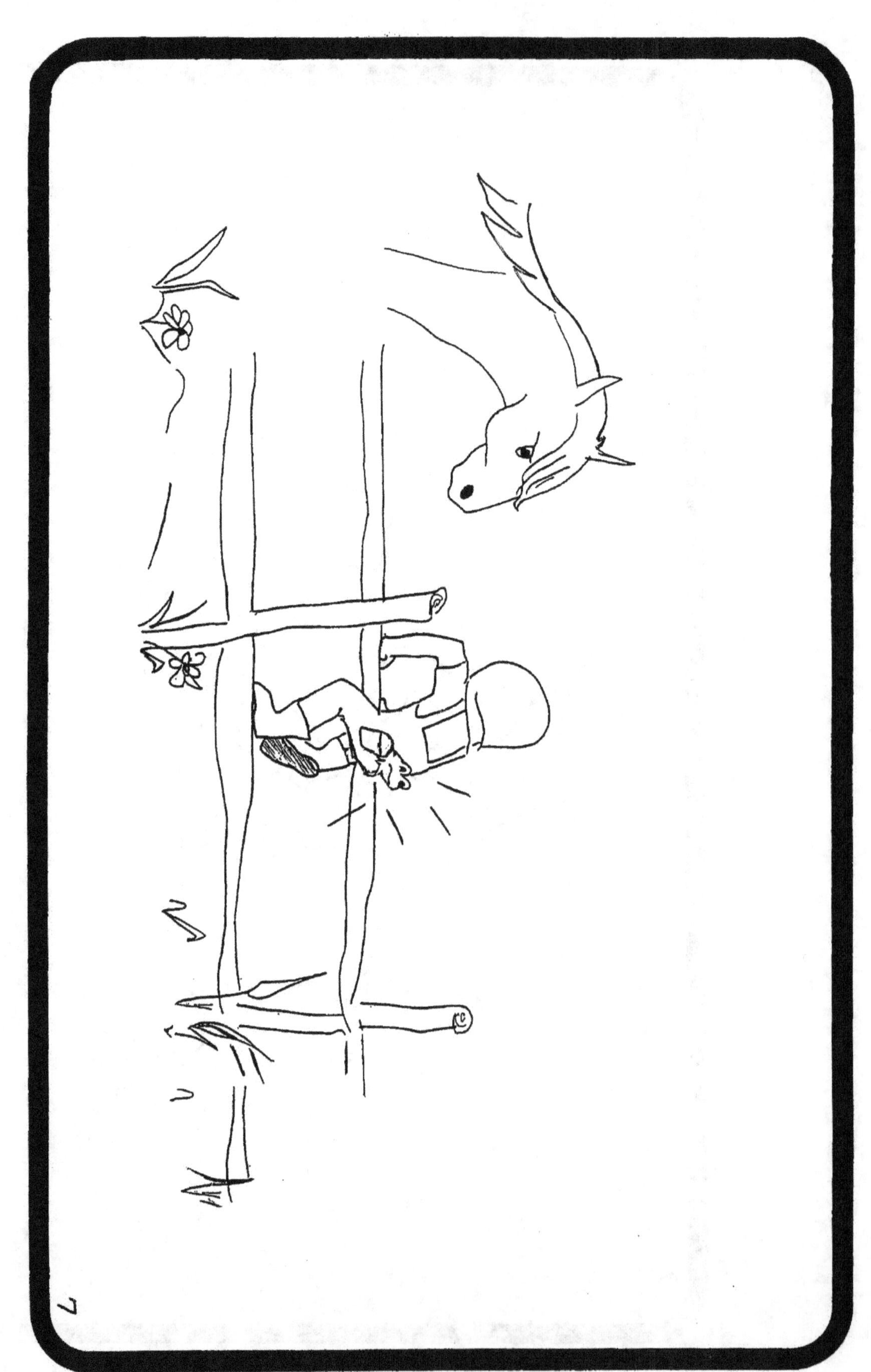

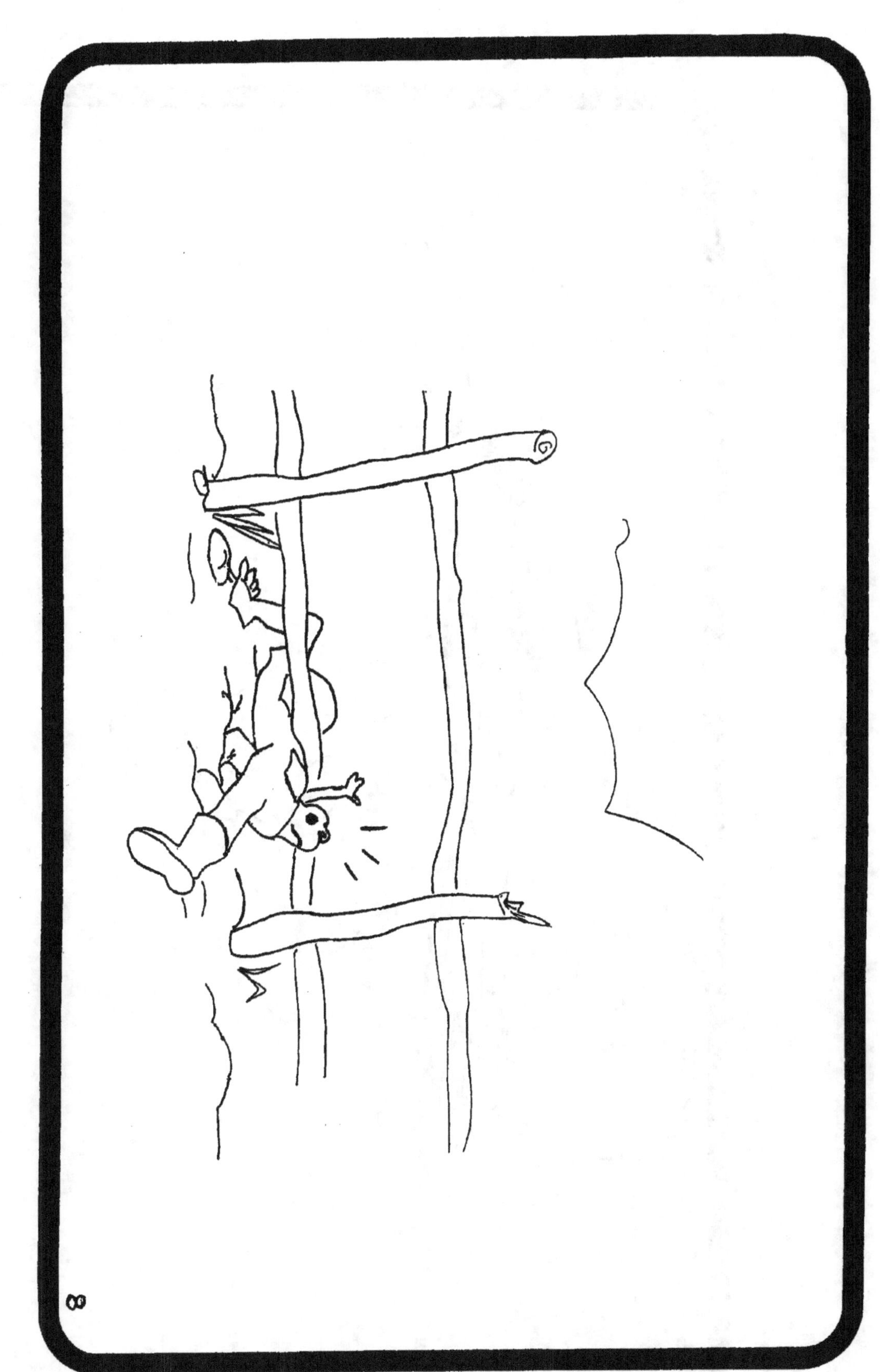

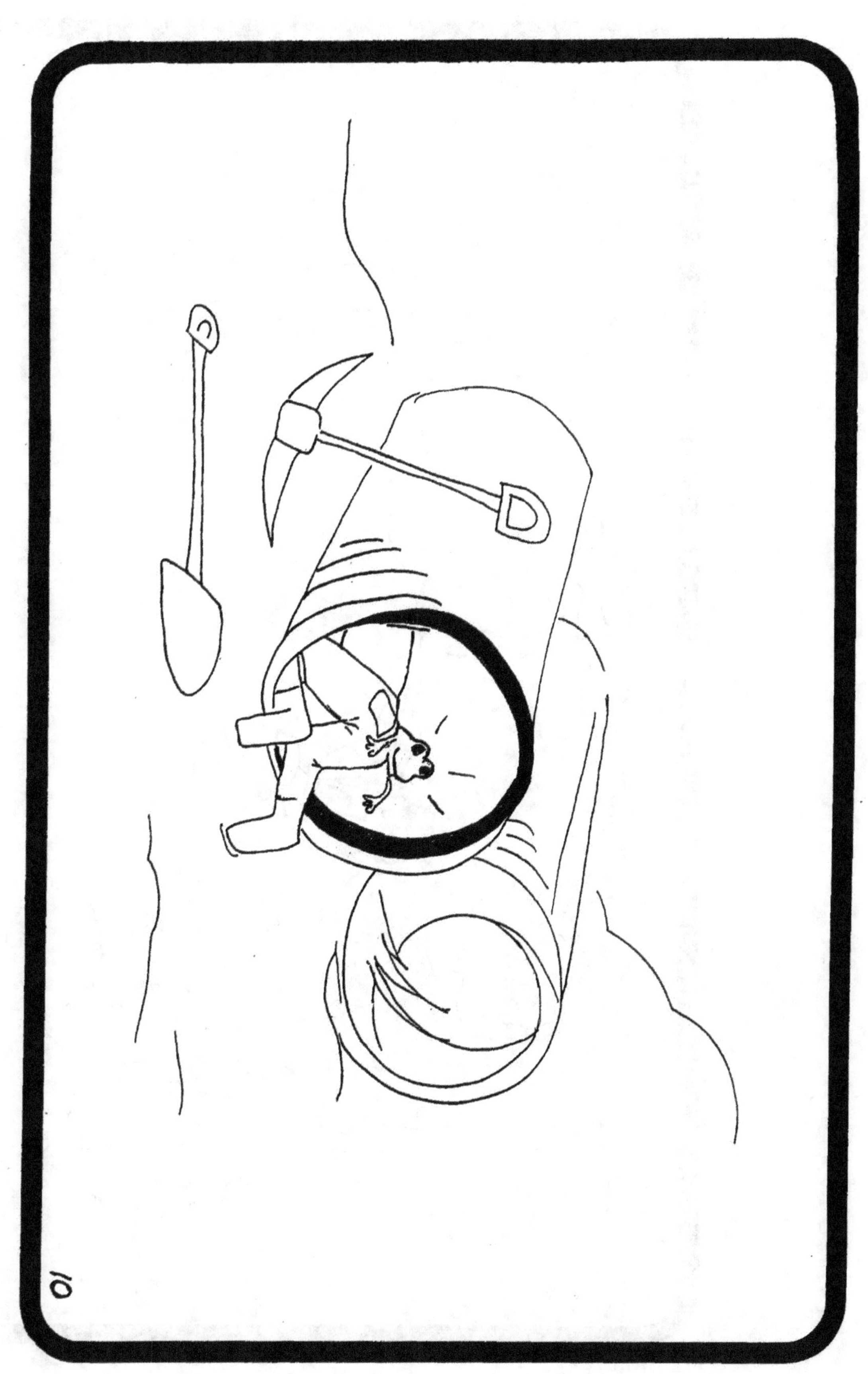

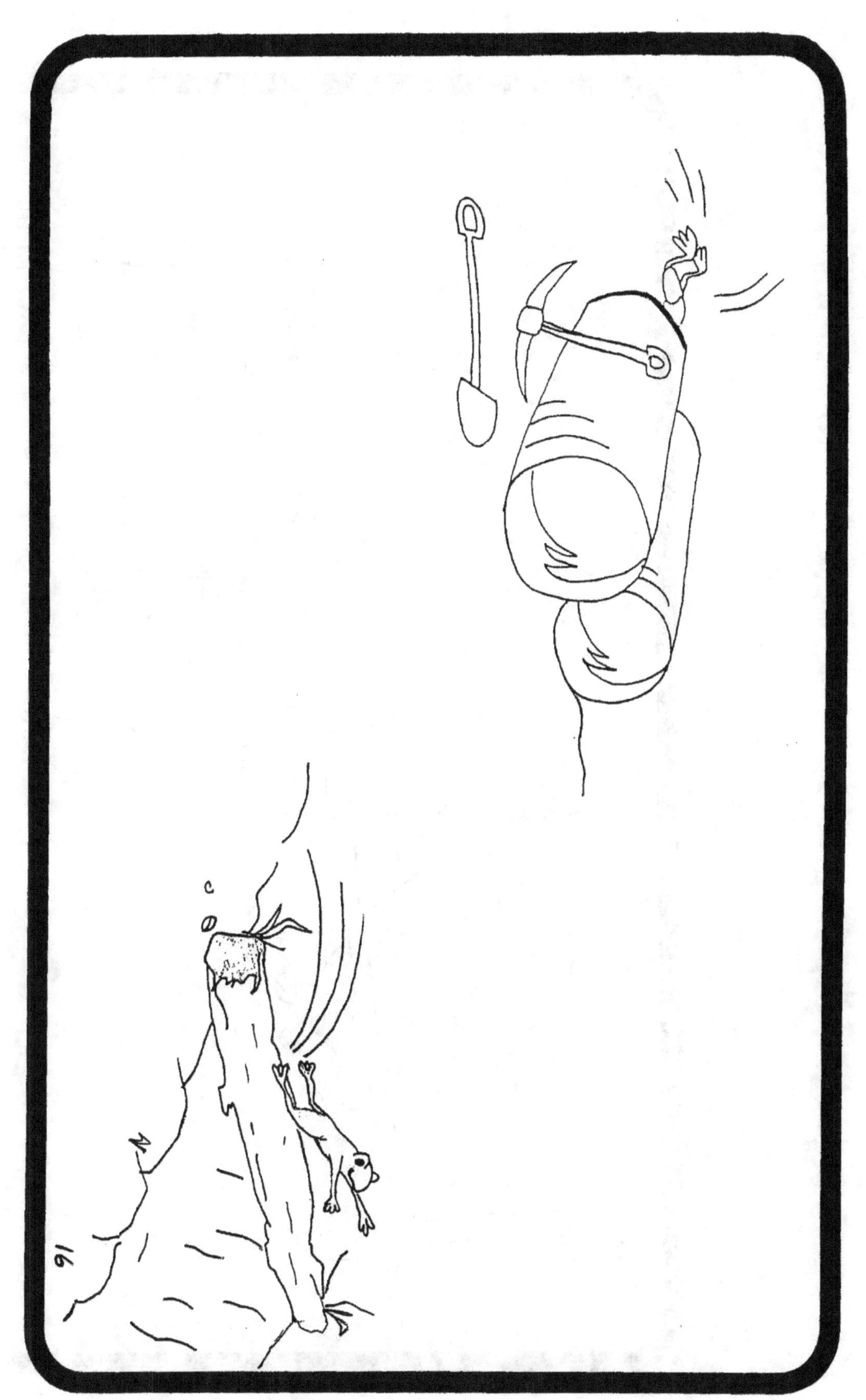

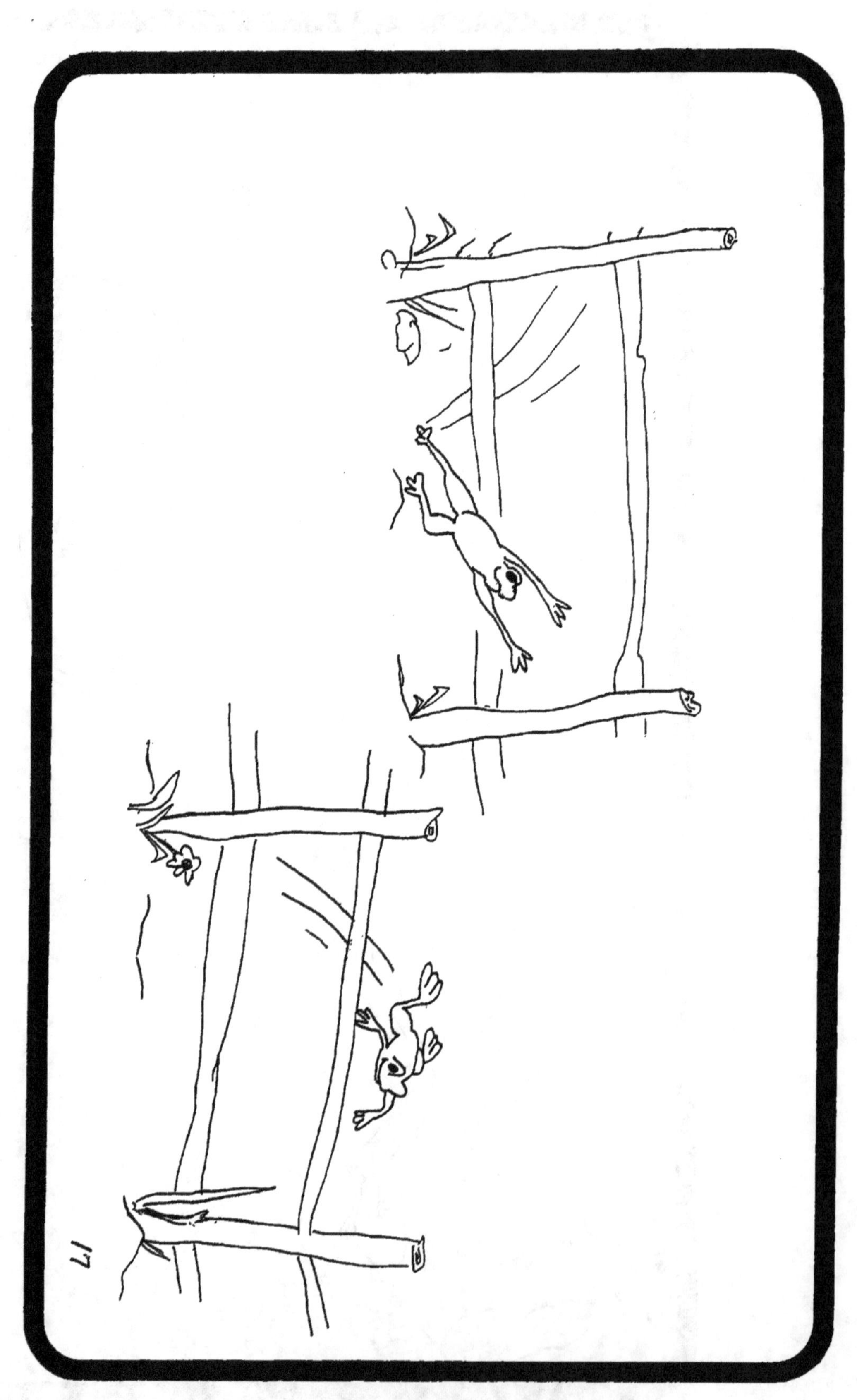

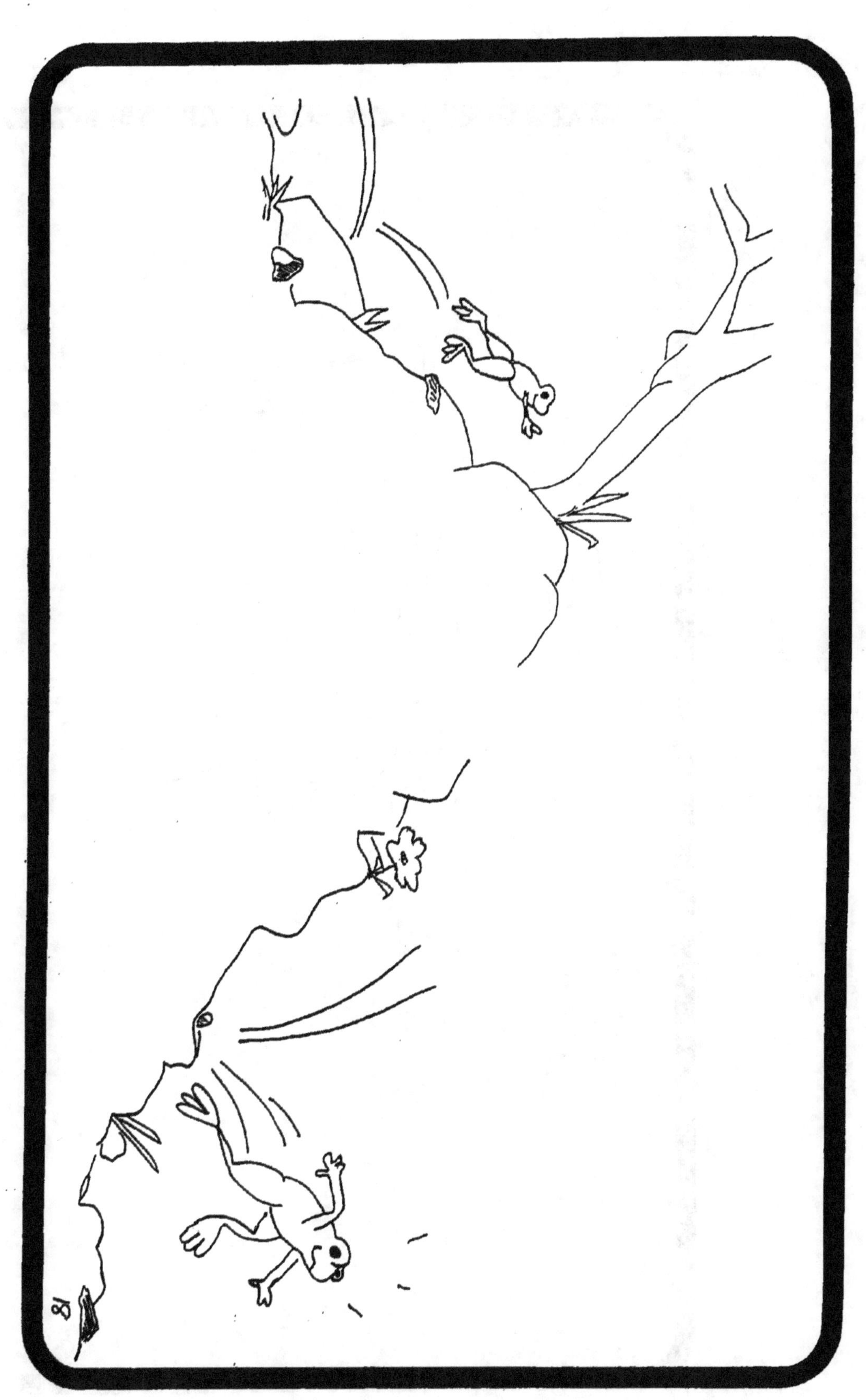

21